38 CENTS

JAYLEN LAGRANDE

Jaylen LaGrande Enterprises
Dallas, Texas
www.JaylenLaGrande.com
jaylen592@yahoo.com

Cover Photography by: Desmond Hunt, Dlores Photography, Dallas, TX

Author Headshot by: Cyndi B, Dallas, TX

Proofread by: Tenita Johnson, So It Is Written, LLC – www.soitiswritten.net

Edited by: L.A. Eaton and Zaharah McKinney

Interior Design & Formatting by: Ya Ya Ya Creative – www.yayayacreative.com

ISBN No. 978-0-9858531-1-2

PRINTED AND BOUND IN THE UNITED STATES OF AMERICA

TO UNCLE LUCKY

†

PRAISE FOR 38 CENTS

A story of faith, ambition and endurance, LaGrande's transparency causes readers to believe in the midst of defeat. This uplifting read celebrates the faith-based entrepreneur and offers advice and comfort—challenging us to hope against hope, and trust the plan of God. This is a must-read for anyone who is struggling with a vision God gave them.

–Dr. Alexis Maston-Mcclinton, Ph.D.
Author, Entrepreneur & Speaker

Written with kingdom visionaries and entrepreneurs in mind, LaGrande challenges us to do what we've been afraid to do for decades: run with revelation. This manuscript offers practical success strategies for harvesting your God-given vision.

–Deon Howard
Blogger for Charisma Magazine *and*
Advisor for Forward Financial Group

Continued

From *fear to faith, pain to purpose* and turmoil to triumph, *38 Cents* captivates our hearts through it's riveting ability to document LaGrande's trailblazing journey to kingdom marketplace success. He transparently exposes his shortcomings to ensure that the generations to follow do not emulate those same mistakes—but learn from the pain he experienced. What an amazingly clear picture of how God-given dreams are actualized and how the favor of God follows the obedient believer.   –Paul K. Ellis, Jr.
Author, When Saints Pray
Lead Pastor, Glory Seekers Church (Ft. Lauderdale, FL)
CEO, Ellis & Ellis Consulting Group, LLC

If you need encouragement on your pursuit of God and His plans in business, I highly recommend this book! Jaylen walks out what he believes with incredible faith and integrity, and God has worked in his business in marvelous ways.

–Page Vandiver, *Entrepreneur*
www.SimplyHeavenDesign.com

Once again, Jaylen has shared his secret to success: perseverance, courage and, above all, faith. Jaylen teaches us how to cloak ourselves with the wetsuit of perseverance and courageously plunge into a new beginning.

–Rhonda Hamilton, *Entrepreneur*

ACKNOWLEDGEMENTS

It's been a long time coming – six years, to be exact – but my third book is finally published and I couldn't be more excited.

First, I'd like to thank my Lord and Savior, Jesus Christ, for all He's done for me. The blessings, the lessons and everything in between.

To my mother, my grandmother, my father, my aunties and uncles, sisters and brothers, cousins, and friends, my 3:16 staff (former and present) and the Power 5 Network: I want to thank you from the bottom of my heart for pushing me.

To my editorial team, Zaharrah, L.A. Eaton and Tenita Johnson: Words can't even begin to express my gratitude for you all. Thanks for continuing to push me.

To every customer who has supported my brands, 3:16 Collection and Religious Expressions, thanks for sowing into the vision, supporting the mission and believing in me.

To every mentor I've had in my life, including Rick Betenbough (Betenbough Homes), Gary Rovarino (Spirit and Truth Jewelry), and even T.D. Jakes (though we haven't met *yet*, I know it's going to happen soon). I truly appreciate every single one of you.

There's a million people I could name, but those that are near and dear know it without having to be acknowledged here. I appreciate each and every single one of you. I couldn't have done any of this without you.

To my readers, I pray you enjoy this literary masterpiece.

Big Love,

Jaylen LaGrande

TABLE OF CONTENTS

Foreword 1

Introduction 3

Dear Reader 7

Chapter One: Holding Back the Flood of Fear 9

Chapter Two: Provision in the Process 17

Chapter Three: Born into Faith 23

Chapter Four: Young Man Becoming 31

Chapter Five: The Weight of the Anointing .41

Chapter Six: Rushed into Purpose 51

Chapter Seven: 38 Cents and a Planted Seed 61

Chapter Eight: A New Level … A New Name 69

Chapter Nine: The Marketplace Mandate 77

Chapter Ten: Thy Kingdom Come 87

Chapter Eleven: Establishing a Kingdom Business 97

Chapter Twelve: Running with Revelation 103

Bonus: Photos of Success 111

About Jaylen 115

Other Books by Jaylen 119

FOREWORD
BY NEVERL KAMBASHA

Let the giant within you rise!

If I were to summarize this book in a sentence, those are the words that come to mind. This book will certainly give you the inspiration and revelation to do just that.

This book will unlock the value that God has already placed inside you. It will profoundly guide you on how to embrace that prophetic call from God. Once you have understood this call, and you allow God to deposit something new into you, all you have to do is sit back and watch God guide your life into a new direction. Watch Him turn your 38 cents into something priceless. This literary masterpiece provides a clear message of faith and overcoming adversity. Most importantly, it expands on an important aspect of Christian faith: marketplace ministry. When you get to the chapter on the marketplace mandate, you will realize that we are *all* called to ministry that goes beyond just the four walls of the church—but we're called to expand that ministry into the marketplace. We can no longer confine ourselves to limited thinking. We need to understand that the further we reach out in our ministry, the more lives we can impact, which is precisely what God has called us to do. God wants us to have dominion over the works of our hands if we would only allow Him to deposit something new into us.

I have known Jaylen for a significant amount of time, and I have watched how God has transformed him into a new man. I have watched how his journey has unfolded and how God has called him to spread the good news through marketplace ministry. There is no better person to learn how to not only think outside the box—but to completely push back on the box that encompasses much of the usual way of being a Christian. Let God birth a new you! You do not need much. This book will guide you on how to answer the call and let that giant within you arise.

Mr. Neverl Kambasha
Founder Beryl Holdings (Pty) Limited
Founder Kingdom Business Network (SA)
Businessman and Philanthropist

INTRODUCTION
BY VANESSA LYNN

> If you have faith as the grain of a mustard seed,
> you will say to this mountain, be thou
> removed and cast in the sea.
> −Luke 17:6

This sounds great! We receive this in churches, mount it on our walls, and get inspirational emails with this very familiar passage of Scripture.

However, most believers don't have the belief, nor the faith, in themselves and, ultimately, in God that they can start and maintain a business. *We walk by faith and not by sight* (2 Corinthians 5:7). This is another familiar passage. But if you are striving to maintain your own empire, this is not just another Scripture. This becomes your *reality*. The truth is that you may have a desire to start or continue your business, but your bank account, credit cards, mortgages and car notes all say something different. Trying to launch out into the deep, you may find little to no support from loved ones, closed doors, rejection letters from banks, or even little to no sales. These are just some of the obstacles we face as entrepreneurs.

Ultimately, after so much rejection, it's natural for the believer to doubt the vision and call to the marketplace. I started my personal journey over two decades ago. I had a love and a passion for decorating special events and weddings. Being an ordained minister, it was also the perfect opportunity to shine my light to my clients. As things blossomed and took off relatively fast, that growth also had its consequences. My lack of training and direction ultimately caused the business to crash. I was forced to close my doors and face public scandal.

As a business owner, we have more than ourselves to contend with. Our decisions affect staff members and others' wellbeing and livelihood. My journey at one time caused me to give up. But when it's in you, it's in you! Nearly a decade later, I found myself with an opportunity to get back into the business. And while I have gone through many transitions, I can say now that I own two banquet facilities in the Metro Detroit area that serve hundreds of families, businesses and ministries annually. And more times than I'd like to admit, the only thing I seem have is *faith*. Many days, I don't see how payroll can be made, or how rent and bills will be taken care of. It's a struggle only few can survive. It's this struggle and calling that connected me with my "nephew," Jaylen LaGrande, who has become one of my closest confidants. Understand that, as in life, there are seasons in business. Some sunshine, some rain. Some things fall, and then they spring again. Having mustard seed faith to move mountains is sometimes the mountains of fear, doubt, self-esteem and lack. Being an entrepreneur in the Kingdom, with all its challenges, puts each of us in a unique position. Not only do we leave a legacy for our families, but it puts us in a position to help guide the destinies of many and to spread the love of Jesus Christ in this cut-throat world of business.

DEAR READER,

I've been in the place you find yourself in right now. Feeling called, but unequipped. Feeling led, but in the dark about how to follow. Having a vision, but unable to clearly see ahead. Fearful of the unknown, yet unable to give up on the very thing God has spoken to your heart.

The tears I've shed, the bricks I've laid, the rivers I've crossed, the bridges I've built, the ceilings I've shattered, the doubts I've crucified, the naysayers I've hushed – I did it for you.

The pain was not in vain. The sleepless nights were worth it to be able to give you a guide to following that which God has ordained and purposed you to do.

The Bible says that we are overcome by the blood of the lamb and the words of our testimony. Often God uses our testimony to reach back and pull others ahead, while inspiring them to propel further into their destinies.

Take these words. Let them speak life. Let them guide you alongside the still, small voice that has been speaking to you.

> Step out on faith. Trust.
> Be intentional. Be bold. Be unapologetic.

Remember, you're not next. Your time is now. It's your time to let your light shine. You are going to change the world. Everything that has happened in your life up until this moment has been a seed planted toward the harvest you are about to walk into. I pray after reading this story, your life will never be the same.

I decree new levels of faith, new dimensions of vision and an abundance of ideas. But, more importantly, I pray that as you read, you'll be reminded just how faithful God is to fulfill the promises He has made to you.

2 Corinthians 1:4-5

CHAPTER ONE
HOLDING BACK
THE FLOOD OF FEAR

> When you pass through the waters,
> I will be with you; and through the rivers,
> they shall not overwhelm you; when you walk
> through fire you shall not be burned,
> and the flame shall not consume you.
> —Isaiah 43:2 (ESV)

DECEMBER 2015

I was consumed with fear of the unknown, my heart pacing fiercely, as I approached the back entrance of the store.

I'd just driven through the remnants of the blizzard that had hit the city a few days before—the adrenaline in my bloodstream only interrupted by the ice water that soaked through my boots, forcing me into a cold shock. I could feel my wet socks squishing inside my boots as I made my way down the long hallway, scared of what I might find at its end. The south end of the mall had collapsed and that was where my store was located.

My pride and joy – *Religious Expressions*. I couldn't bring myself to think of the potential damage incurred. I turned the key, opened the back door of my store, and was met with rushing water. I went straight to the electric panel and flicked all 30 switches in attempt to get power and bring sight to my new reality. I approached the door between my stockroom and the sales floor, looked down, and found my worst fears confirmed.

The store was submerged in water.

All my fixtures, equipment and merchandise was drowning by nearly three feet. My disbelief and shock fell from my eyes as tears, disappearing into the water on the floor. As I looked into the puddles, I could see my face, reflecting back to me the year of struggle I had endured. The pain began to grip me. My confidence was engulfed in the water that now stood between me and that which I "believed" was an answer to prayer.

All I could think was, *Another flood? Again?*

Yep. Twice in one year. Only this time, it hit twice as hard.

The beginning of the year had brought a piping issue in the mall, which caused raw sewage to flood my entire store. I lost everything. The insurance company only covered so much because I hadn't done proper due diligence in understanding my coverages. Because of my disregard for the details, I had endured an unnecessary year of struggle and pain.

> Trust that God's plan would prevail and take us from trial to triumph!

My store experienced a huge financial decline as the sewage flood caused a ripple effect in every aspect of my business. The health of my store deteriorated as we experienced loss of merchandise and a six-week closure. To make matters worse, a recent real estate battle with a national retailer had resulted in a move to the "slow end" of the mall, and the consequence was slow foot traffic. With no money left in savings, and no compensation from the insurance company, things were looking extremely bleak.

I had to do what I knew best, which was to trust that God's plan would prevail and take us from trial to triumph. I would utilize my entrepreneurial know-how that I'd developed from an early age, and maximize every resource the best that I could. I had to be creative in my endeavors. Yet, I was bound by the natural fear of the unknown, and the lack of assurance for any potential solution. All I could do was take things a day at a time.

With every month that passed that year, I grew further behind on rent payments with the mall. I couldn't keep the shelves properly stocked and my creativity was paralyzed by the thoughts that consumed me. It became harder, impossible even, to make payroll. The letters and calls from debt collectors and vendors requesting payment on past due invoices only ignited my anxieties. I grew overwhelmed trying to figure out how to keep the doors open and overcome this setback.

I knew I was called to this venture. But, the weight of the struggles and roadblocks in my way made me doubt my calling on many occasions. The only force that kept me moving forward was the fact that ministry within the store was at its peak. While it had been the toughest year for me financially, and business was at an all-time low, we'd reached more people that year through our store bible studies, worship nights and day-to-day customer interactions. Our location in the mall was not the best for business, but the huge space allowed for large groups of people.

That year, I had to really take God at His word. It became vital that I practice what I preached and encouraged those around me to believe. My faith was being tested and it was imperative that I trust God like never before. But with so much disappointment, and so many attacks from the enemy, against me and my ministry, it became tougher to believe that my employees and I would see our way through.

After nearly four months of being behind on rent, the mall manager had done pretty much all she could to buy me time to recuperate. Despite the small payments I had been making, our delinquency became more intense. She was willing to work with me because she knew the dramatic effect the sewage flood had on our business. But there was only so much she could do at the local level. Once it reached the corporate level, they demanded that she collect the past-due rent. Because we were six months behind, a 30-day eviction notice was served.

I had to pay or vacate the premises.

My stress levels were already through the roof. I was ready to throw in the towel. But my faith would not grant my waver.

There were days I had to take five dollars from my store register just to scrape up something to eat. I became delinquent on my car note, trying to ensure that I made payroll so my employees wouldn't feel the weight of the store's struggles. I vividly remember the repossession guy calling to warn me that he was outside to get my car. I begged him to pretend that he couldn't find it, and asked him to give me a few more days to come up with the money. Even after a deferment, it was hard for me to keep my car note up-to-date. What mattered was keeping my store open so I could continue ministry at the mall, even if that meant putting my personal bills on the back burner.

During this year, I realized what was important and what wasn't. I realized what mattered and what didn't matter. I realized that it was bigger than me. The proof came when I turned down job offers, investors and opportunities that would benefit me personally. I instead focused on continuing to build my company.

Continuing to spread the gospel and encourage those who came into the store was what was most important. My ambitions as an entrepreneur took a back seat. In this moment, I realized the bigger picture: to spark a global movement of God in the marketplace.

Through all of the struggles, I believed in what I was called to do and I wasn't going to allow anything to stop me from pursuing it.

An investor approached me about the business and suggested I give up my physical store front. He wanted me to commit to selling online only and focus on developing products and selling wholesale to other stores. I turned it down because I knew the importance of the physical store. Having a brick and mortar gave us the opportunity to reach people we wouldn't be able to reach through online channels or selling to other stores. Being out in the community is what set us apart.

No matter the setbacks, I stood firm, steadfast and unmovable—knowing that somehow, some way, we would make it out of this storm.

> And let us not grow weary of doing good,
> for in due season we will reap,
> if we do not give up.
> —Galatians 6:9

I meditated on this verse day and night, reminding myself that if God brought me to it, He would bring me through it. I held on because I knew that every trial and storm has an expiration date and, like the old song by Timothy Wright says, "Trouble don't last always."

When I was served with the first eviction notice, the dire nature of the situation became so real that I felt I had truly hit rock bottom. I scraped up enough to buy me another 30 days—twice. What I came to find was that, while the struggles taught me lessons, it wasn't where God dwelt. He was *in* the blessings in the lessons, blessings that would soon propel me to go forward into something even greater.

I'll never forget the day I was sitting in the store, trying to figure out if I should just pack up and go. I wondered if I should save face from the embarrassment of being locked out of my store, or if I should just cry out to God one more time and ask for a sign. As I cried out in that moment for a sign, I had to trust that God was listening and ready to show up in a mighty way.

CHAPTER TWO
PROVISION IN THE PROCESS

The Holy Spirit has such an intentional way of providing for you what you need, just when you need it the most. One particular day, when I was contemplating my impending failure, a couple I'd never met came into the store to shop. They were so excited about the store that they bought over $200 worth of products, a considerable amount given the fact that we barely had any stock on the shelves.

It has become my practice to refrain from telling customers that I own the store. I don't want my title to influence their experience. (I'd realized early on that it was never *about me*, but about what God wanted to do *through me*). After the couple left the store, I was getting ready to lock up and saw them turn back around. Once they approached the doorway, the husband asked if I owned the store. After I confirmed, he began to speak encouragement to me. It was as if life began entering a place of dead dreams.

He reminded me that God loved me, and that everything I was facing was just preparing me for my next level; that no matter how hard things may have seemed, it was important to never give up.

> It was never *about me*, but about what God wanted to do *through me*.

Then the wife interrupted. "We have something for you. It's a gift." She smiled. "As my husband and I were leaving the store, the Holy Spirit prompted us to turn around and come back to give this to you." She pulled out her checkbook and wrote me a check for $1,000 with these simple instructions: "Pay your tithes and trust God to bring forth every provision you need to take your business to the next level."

This was September of 2015. From that day through December of that year, I witnessed the miracle of people coming together to bring me out of the financial rut that had swallowed my business.

After being behind nearly $30,000 in rent, God provided. After facing three different eviction letters that year, I was able to bring the rent current just three days before Christmas. Strangers showed up day after day to sow into Religious Expressions, without even knowing the severity of the debt that we were facing. Despite a nearly 60 percent decline in holiday sales over past years, we had prevailed. I had been humbled into the understanding that it was *not by might, nor by power, but by the Spirit of the Lord* (Zechariah 4:6).

God sent so many people to encourage me and help keep my head up, even when I wanted to give up. It was almost as though He had assigned others to remind me that I was in the right place. Even though it didn't seem that things were lining up, I trusted God to get me through.

But now, here I was, three days away from the year ending. Less than a week after I'd finally brought my rent up to speed, and I felt like I was right back where I'd started. The past year, I had experienced so many ups and downs from the sewage flood that caused a chain reaction of setbacks. I'd finally caught up. I was finally back on track. I had faced stress, depression, frustration and eviction several times and persevered ... *or so I thought!* Here I was, walking into another flood, that was even worse than the first. I had a whole new set of problems!

The news outlets labeled the disaster an "act of God." As if that wasn't enough, the blizzard was named Goliath. While people were calling me a man after God's own heart, like David, I felt nothing of the sort, standing in that the water that was flushing away my dreams. I only felt as though my giant, Goliath, had defeated me and wiped me out.

In 1 Samuel 17, the Bible talks about a young Israelite named David, who was called by King Saul to battle a

Philistine named Goliath. The Bible describes Goliath as a giant with full armor. In this story, David (just a young boy) was sent to fight someone much bigger than him, in what seemed to be an impossible battle. And yet, it was because he was called by God that he had favor on his side. He was able to kill the giant and win freedom for his land. What looked impossible to onlookers became possible because, although he wasn't equipped for this battle externally, internally, he had everything he needed to conqueror his enemy.

It was at this moment that my thoughts told me that everything I'd pressed through that year had been in vain. Perhaps I'd ignored the signs that it was time for me to admit defeat. Perhaps my ambition had clouded what God *really* wanted me to do.

Standing in that water, I finally released myself from my own plans and reflected on the previous four years of business. I thought about all the good times and bad times. After taking a deep dive into all my fears, sorrows and doubts, I realized the reason my year had come full circle. God had finally released me to a new level of "greater" and everything that had happened prior to the flood (good and bad) had only prepared me for what God was about to do next in my life. It's like school. Once you successfully master things on the grade level you're on, you graduate to a new level.

In a way, the flood was nothing more than an answer to my prayers. Like the story of Noah's Ark, the flood came to cleanse the old and bring forth the new. Everything I had faced in my business previously needed to be separated from what I was about to walk into. A bigger platform. A bigger calling. A bigger anointing. Greater power and greater influence. A global impact on the world.

> God had finally released me to a new level of "greater".

Oftentimes, the things we are praying for don't always come in the package we expect them to, but it doesn't mean God isn't listening to us or answering our prayers. I've read before that the things we fear the most are usually the things we need. In that moment, I knew I could no longer hold my fears at bay. I could no longer escape the fear. Things were lining up, and the flood was merely a blessing in disguise, a release into new beginnings. We so often identify trials and struggles as attacks from the enemy when, more often than not, it's God's way of realigning us. He's preparing us for something greater than we've ever imagined.

CHAPTER THREE
BORN INTO FAITH

> In the same way, let your light shine before others, so that they may see your good works and give glory to your Father who is in heaven.
> —Matthew 5:16

My grandma shares the story of my birth every chance she gets. It's become a special part of my life. Even as a young child, I loved to hear Grandma tell the story of my entry to the world. As a grown man, I realize how truly blessed I am to have this direct connection to her. I also realize how bittersweet it must be for her to constantly relive that time.

You see, it was an occasion of life, as well as death. It was one of the toughest seasons of Grandma's life. On a Sunday, June 14th, 1992 – a little over three weeks after I came into this world – she lost her eldest daughter, my Aunt Toni, to aggressive colon cancer. My aunt died at the Cancer Treatment Center of America in Zion, Illinois. Most people will say that if they could have one wish, it would be that they are returned to God before their children because there is no experience so unimaginably painful as losing a child. My grandma found that out firsthand and the pain was excruciating. Her sorrow overcame her so much that her second oldest daughter had to pull her away from the bedside to leave the hospital. And while incredibly difficult to leave her baby's side, it was time for Grandma to board the plane that would return her home to Detroit, Michigan.

Filled with sorrow and exhausted from the trip, she noticed there seemed to be a lot of traffic as she pulled up to her home. There were cars parked up and down her street and people coming in and out of her house. Friends and family had gathered from afar to support and console her.

When she opened the doors of the house, she was met with a crowd of people who had congregated in her living room. She could hear the sounds of quiet conversations. She could smell the food that

"This child is anointed and is going to do great things."

people had cooked. She felt the arms around her as each person met her with warm embrace. Others had come to clean house and ensure that Grandma had everything she needed to be comforted at such a trying time.

As she walked into the dining room, sad, yet grateful, she saw a white bassinet lying underneath the window. Walking closer, rays of sunlight beamed from the window onto that bassinet and bounced off the baby's skin. When she got halfway toward the window, she audibly heard the Holy Spirit speak to her: "This child is anointed and is going to do great things."

I was that baby, and every year my Grandma tells me:

"This was my first time meeting you, my ninth grandchild, and I'll never forget that day. Even on one of the toughest days of my life, and with so many people gathered to comfort me, I'll forever take delight in knowing that God spoke to me concerning you. It gave me a comfort and peace that surpassed all understanding. Every chance I get, I'll forever remind you to walk upright in the anointing God placed on your life."

I must have been anxious to begin my life and to meet my Auntie Toni before she departed because I was born much earlier than anticipated. I like to believe that God orchestrated that just right because He allowed her to be present and involved in the beginning of my life, even as she was nearing the end of hers. In fact, all four of my aunties were involved. I was born prematurely while my mom was vacationing in sunny California. So everyone rushed to help and welcome me. Auntie Toni stood next to my mother's bedside as she delivered me. With a big smile on her face, my auntie cut the cord and released me into the world.

Although I have no recollection of my aunt because I was only three weeks old when she passed away, her legacy will always be a part of me. People still talk about how she was always the life of the party and how she always brought such positive energy into the room. I often hear about how her smile would light up the night and she was always there to encourage others and lend a helping hand. I like to think the light in my life was a direct inheritance from her.

At the time, my auntie Rhonda wanted to name me "Sunshine." Though I'm glad that didn't happen, all of these things remind me of the mandate God placed on my life. God's will was that my light always shine brightly, and that I may be an example to the world that with a measure of faith, obedience and purpose, anything is possible through Jesus Christ.

THROUGH THE EYES OF A CHILD

I seemed to understand what my purpose was very early on in age. My mom says that, as a young child, I continually brought light and hope into her life, without really knowing what I was doing. I was able to speak encouraging words to her during some of her darkest days. She was consistently amazed at my ability to reassure her and uplift her spirits with my words.

Even before I was old enough to read, there were times I would recite Scripture to her or share Bible stories I'd learned, totally unaware of what she was going through. The timeliness and wisdom of my reminders always seemed beyond my years. It warms my heart to know that God saw fit to use me, even as a little boy.

MY FIRST PULPIT

One day, when I was seven years old, an idea came to me and I was inspired to act.

> I've always had a burning desire to encourage people, uplift people, and share the goodness of God

I first went to the utility closet, dragged the vacuum cleaner out into the living room, then climbed the kitchen counters to retrieve masking tape atop the refrigerator. I then grabbed my sister's white karaoke machine and microphone, tying the microphone to the handle of the vacuum cleaner.

Realizing the microphone was still too high for me to reach, I brought the step stool from the kitchen and placed it in front of the ottoman. Standing on the stool, gazing over the microphone, I knew it was perfect. I had created my first pulpit.

Soon after, I invited the neighborhood kids over as I preached my first sermon and my voice boomed through the karaoke machine. I don't know what I said, or even what prompted me to create a way to minister. But ever since I can remember, I've always had a burning desire to encourage people, uplift people, and share the goodness of God.

I would wake up each Sunday, anticipating putting on my suit and going to church, so delighted to learn. I remember when all the other kids wanted to play "house," I wanted to play "church." Beyond that, I loved going to school and was always ready to share the Bible stories I learned with other kids. My grandma always had us in church, but I never felt dragged or forced. While no one ever told me that I had to attend, or that it was wrong not to, I was always eager to go. I always had a passion to learn more. There was just something about the music that moved me. And hearing the preacher break down the Bible stories so eloquently made me feel like a part of the narratives he shared. It was almost as if I had been transported back into biblical times to witness this rich history that meant so much for me. I couldn't get enough.

My uncle Tracy called me "Rev." because every time he saw me, I had a new revelation for him. There was always something about the gospel that excited me. Even before I ever learned to read, the Word of God had already found a place in my heart. Many times, I could recite Scriptures and passages I never studied, but somehow learned. I naturally soaked up the teachings of the Holy Spirit, and the words would come to me when I needed them most. Whether for myself, or to encourage someone else, I was able to comfort and inspire. My desire to encourage others always extended beyond the four walls of the church. Even as a young child, I felt compelled to share the Scriptures that took root in my heart with others. The Word of God gave me confidence that anything was possible.

YOUNG ENTREPRENEUR

I created my first business at eight years old. I remember dragging everything from my model car collection down to the basement of our home. I gathered all my dad's flashlights, every box I could find, and my sister's pink disco ball. I hung the flashlights from the ceiling as best I could and propped up flashlights underneath homemade tables made of cardboard boxes covered with pillowcases. With the disco ball as my centerpiece, I'd created my own homemade auto show.

My fascination with cars bore fruit to a full display of models, from Model T's to Chevrolets. I blame part of that on my grandpa, and the other part on the mere fact that I was raised in Detroit, also known as The Motor City. I remember going through the neighborhood, letting all the kids know I was opening my own auto show and admission would be a quarter. I made $1.75 that day. The entrepreneur inside of me was born and, from that day forward, I was a self-made businessman.

I've always loved business. I loved being able to encourage and inspire people. Everywhere I went, you would find me wearing my little suit, carrying my Bible and my leather briefcase.

Early on in life, it was obvious that I had two major passions: I wanted to be a successful entrepreneur, and I wanted to minister. As I grew and enjoyed childhood, it was evident that God continued to water the seeds of those aspirations. He would always provide. Soon, He showed me that I didn't have to choose. I could do both.

CHAPTER FOUR
YOUNG MAN BECOMING

People will look at a successful business man or woman, and assume that they got to where they are overnight. But there is always a story behind the journey. There are identifiable qualities of a budding entrepreneur that you may see in yourself or others. These tendencies may show up early in life. But we often look past them because no one is around to cultivate them. Many times, the people around us aren't sure how to encourage and support us.

> The anointing that God often marks on our lives cannot be comprehended simply.

Since the age of five, God was preparing me for the work that I would complete in my lifetime. Many people have tried to understand the calling on my life and dissect it into terms they could understand on their individual levels. But the anointing that God often marks on our lives cannot be comprehended that simply. It reaches beyond the surface of what people often see with the human eye.

IN THE BIG LITTLE LEAGUES

It may have happened to you at a young age or has yet to happen to you in your adult years. But when you follow your heart, your passion will identify your calling. I was 11 years old when my mom drove me downtown to register my first business. I opened a bank account, signed up my first client (a lawn maintenance service), and just like that, *Jay's Card Designs* began.

It all started with designing business cards and flyers for friends and family. As my clientele grew, word of mouth caught like wildfire. Suddenly, I was designing business cards for all types of companies. One day, I was in Big Lots with my mom. I was elated to find greeting card paper and templates on the clearance rack. I bought the entire stock— nearly 30 packs of 24 cards. After going through two entire packs on trial and error (in some ways, I'm a perfectionist), I launched *Card-Works 3000*, a division of *Jay's Card Designs*. That was the first time I truly saw my passions merging. I was able to mix my passion for writing, ministry and business all into one.

In today's society, we often make decisions based on what we think we should do or what others think we should do. Money, or the lack of it, often dictates what path we take. We are taught we must work a nine-to-five job with benefits, no matter whether we enjoy it or not, just so we can pay the bills and keep a good credit rating. All that is important. But if you listen to what your heart is saying, you will find your calling. You'll be just as successful as, or even more so, than that soul-draining job you were advised to take. Of course as a child, no one was trying to hire me in the corporate world. But it was important to me to listen to what my inner being was asking for. My cards were not just custom greeting cards or a project meant to keep a young man busy. My words inspired and gave others hope. I personally received great joy and healing through writing those cards. Eventually, I went into making custom gift bags and brochures, and I had a full print shop—all self-taught on Microsoft Publisher.

If money wasn't an option, what would you do? What kinds of dreams did you have as a child? Look deep inside and find what makes your heart sing.

INTO THE TEENAGE YEARS

I walked through the school hallways, passing out my business cards with a certain confidence. In a way, I was commanding my space in commerce, even in my youth. But behind that self assurance were my middle and high school teachers, who often expressed their impression for my business acumen. You will find people in your life who will support your dreams, even if they sound crazy to some. And some of your biggest fans will know your potential even before you do. Somehow, I suspect my parents knew.

When it came to Christmas, I didn't ask for the usual gifts most kids asked for under the tree. I was more interested in things that would improve my business. At twelve years old, I begged my mom and dad to buy me a glass top desk. I thought that desk was the best thing since sliced bread. That Christmas changed my life.

I walked into the living room that morning, enjoying the beautiful sight. The tree was lit with white lights and purple and silver ornaments that draped perfectly from its branches. Underneath were beautiful boxes; some wrapped in silver and some wrapped in purple. The silver presents were for me, and everything in purple was for my little sister, Ashley.

After opening my PlayStation 2, a few outfits, some cars to add to my model car collection, and a few others, I settled down to enjoy my gifts. But then my mom and dad brought out three more boxes that changed the trajectory of my mindset. Inside those three boxes were my glass top desk, a file cabinet and a brand new HP Printer. I know that doesn't sound very exciting to the typical teenager, but I was set beside myself with joy. It was the executive package that made everything feel so official. It's what propelled me even further into my entrepreneurial ambitions.

Wanting and getting those gifts was also a confirmation for me that it was alright to be different than everyone else. Celebrate your individuality and embrace your uniqueness. This life is a gift and God wants you to use your talents to live the best one you can.

> Some of your biggest fans will know your potential even before you do.

I eventually slowed down my momentum with *Jay's Card Designs* and went on to other ventures. But that experience was invaluable as it set my business adventure into full force.

EVIDENCE OF THE APOSTOLIC MANDATE

Your life is full of instances and experiences that indicate what you have a passion for. If you look back, you'll see evidence of your true becoming. When I was 13 years old, Ashley, my cousin Toni, and I started our own television show called *Talent Search*. Using a camcorder I'd received for my birthday one year prior, we created an avenue to showcase our talents. We draped a sheet from the ceiling and used the mattress as our stage for our production. My sister danced, my cousin Toni sang, and I recited original poetry.

Although *Talent Search* never took off, it ignited my passion for entrepreneurship even further. Because we needed to find ways to raise money to produce the series, I was pushed to be creative beyond measure.

Talent Search went beyond creating content – we hosted bake sales a few times a year where we baked and sold all kinds of desserts. My grandmother's house was on a main street with a lot of traffic, which was perfect to set up our outside table of wares.

This is where I learned marketing and management. I had to market our bake sales throughout the community. I gathered all my friends and the neighborhood kids to help me pass out flyers. I then marketed to all the members at my church. It got to the point that the local firefighters and police officers would radio each other to come and support our causes. I learned management because I was in charge of every aspect, from the back-end kitchen to the front-end sales. Every year, we managed to fork in a few hundred bucks per bake sale, which, as kids, excited us to the core.

> You see, *faith* is part belief *and* part works.

I even hosted my own Mother's Day brunch every year for a few years to show appreciation to all the wonderful ladies in my life. It was my way of giving back to all my aunties, great aunts, mom and grandmother. I've always had a certain love for creating events that bring people together.

THE GENESIS OF RELIGIOUS EXPRESSIONS

If you plant a seed of corn, you don't dig it up the next day to see if it started to grow. You water it. You weed it. You give it time to enjoy the sunshine. It's the same with goals. The 3:16 Collection clothing store that you know and love today started as a tiny seed that needed lots of sunshine.

While traveling to Los Angeles, California with my Auntie Rhonda in the summer of 2009, I stumbled across a store in the wholesale district where I purchased two dozen Christian-themed t-shirts with various messages.

I didn't realize it at the time, but this would become the first seed planted toward the 3:16 Collection that everyone knows and loves today.

I went back to Detroit, wearing one of the shirts, and became a walking billboard to evangelize the gospel. What started as a way to boldly profess my faith turned into my next business venture. People wanted these shirts. As demand grew, I had to figure out exactly how to supply.

My *faith* has always been the *key* to opening doors in my life. I remember ordering dozens of shirts on COD terms, knowing I didn't have the funds. But I was courageous enough to order them because of my trust in Him. I then worked to sell what I had ordered so that I could pay for the COD shipment by the time it arrived at my door. You see, *faith* is part belief *and* part works.

I eventually went on to set up tables at various trade shows and church bazaars. While business was great, ministry was even greater because these were more than just shirts. They were testaments of faith. They were proclamations. They gave people like me a way to express their hearts, and they even sparked conversations, which later led to salvation for some.

In 2009, my last year of high school, my business class was assigned to write a full business plan for a fictitious business. I chose to write a business plan for *Religious Expressions* and describe the details for opening an actual storefront. It was exciting because though, at the time, I never had any intention on ever opening a store, the research process was informative and exhilarating for me. It fed into the formal side of my natural business skills.

> One of the biggest revelations I've received in my life is that our gift is not what we do. It's who we are.

I ended up getting 100 percent on my business plan. I tucked it underneath the bed in a shoe box and continued to move further in growing and becoming.

This was also the year I wrote myself a check for 6.8 million dollars, placed it on my wall, and declared that I would be able to cash that check at age 26. At the time of writing this book, I am 24 years old. But I like to think I am well on my way to seeing that declaration manifest. Believe me, it's not about the money; more importantly, it's about the mandate on my life. I know God is going to use me and my experiences to birth other millionaires and billionaires in the earth realm to equip us with all the provision we need to manifest God's will on earth as it is in heaven.

REFLECTIONS ON THE JOURNEY SO FAR

One of the biggest revelations I've received in my life is that our gift is not what we do. It's who we are. When I reflect on my journey, I realize that entrepreneurship has always been who I am, not what I do. It's truly a calling; something embedded in my being since before my existence. I often meet people in various seasons of my life that have a shortsighted perspective of who I am. They tend to judge me based on my current successes. They don't realize that the victories I walk in today are only a result of a lifetime of seeds and harvest, trials and triumphs, loss and gains, and lessons and blessings.

I've often sat and reflected on my childhood. I am always amazed at how tenacious I was and how I always stepped out so easily to pursue the dreams within me. That childlike faith I possessed, and the innocence of my youth, had me in a place where I didn't doubt things. If I believed I could do it, I would just do it. It's interesting how, as children, our imaginations take us places where we wouldn't dare tread in adulthood. It's interesting to see how we allow society and those around us to infiltrate our minds and hold us back from our very destinies.

I think about how my confidence was so strong, and how what I didn't know allowed me to take leaps and bounds and, ultimately, have so many victories as a young man. I don't boast about this to say I was any different than any other kid. But as I reflect, I am reminded that I was created for this. Success is part of my DNA. Even though things started easily and happened so naturally, I still had a process to endure. Ultimately, this shaped me into who I needed to be. God knew that when my struggles did arrive, I'd always have my experiences as a *young man becoming* to look back on and propel me into the man I would soon be.

CHAPTER FIVE
THE WEIGHT OF THE ANOINTING

> Life is a process, as is every element within it.
> Growth is a process. Education is a process.
> Fitness is a process, and even reaching
> our goals is a process.
>
> The process is often two-sided.

If you train at the gym with the goal to increase strength and muscle mass, you must lift weights. To produce muscle, you must apply a load of stress greater than what your body or muscles had previously adapted to. That means picking up a greater load. Yes, it causes strain, and yes, it is often painful. But the only way to grow is to push past your comfort zone. Every time you press past it, though your muscles are tearing down, the building process brings them back stronger, healthier and bigger than before. By picking up a greater weight, we are able to carry more.

Being called by God for a specific purpose, being anointed, means enduring a process much like that of lifting weights. There are times of strain, pain, feeling broken down and being tired beyond measure. But one must press through the trials to develop a deeper strength. At the end of every tussle, there is a greater strength that is developed that launches you closer to your destiny each time.

Everything that has ever been deemed great started off as a small seed. It had to go through a process in order to reach its full potential—including you and me. We often envy another's success, or view someone else's harvest as plentiful, without considering the process they underwent to get there.

Being called by God means that, beyond what others may deem as effortless, lies a life of selfless sacrifice. If we knew the trials behind what others go through to reach the places where we see them, we would have a deeper appreciation and find encouragement when matters seem to go bleak.

> To truly walk in the fullness of who we are,
> we often have to face both negative and
> positive forces. The attitude we carry
> when things are bad often determine
> how long we remain in the same place.

Personally, I tend to share the good things about my life very naturally. But when the bad occurs, it's difficult to let people in on those vulnerable parts of myself. What I've learned is that, when we are transparent with our own struggles and trials, not only does it allow others to be there for us—but it also allows others to see our human nature and be encouraged as they press on in their own. As they work through their goals, visions and dreams, they are not alone in their struggles, doubts and fears.

I recall so many times looking up to other people for what they had, thinking I'd never arrive to my place of destiny because of all the things I had to endure. I didn't realize that everyone has a story behind their journey. Life is more about the journey than anything because, even when you arrive to new levels and heights, there is always another adventure that lies ahead. Each new level requires a new level of ourselves, and we will always be in a process – no matter how high we are elevated in this life.

THE STORY OF JOSEPH

One of my favorite characters in the Bible is Joseph. To me, his story is so profound and shows us that God is sovereign, even amidst evil, and that He is always with us as we endure the process.

In Genesis Chapter 37-50, we read of a young man named Joseph, son of Jacob. Joseph was his dad's favorite, and his brothers despised him for that fact.

Even at the early age of 17, Joseph was a visionary and dreamer. He told his brothers and his father of a dream he had where Joseph saw his brothers bowing before him as he was ruling over them. This caused his brothers to hate him even more.

His brothers went out into the field and plotted to kill Joseph, with only his oldest brother Ruben objecting. They instead decided to sell him into slavery, deceiving their father to believe that Joseph had been devoured by vicious animals.

Joseph was taken to Egypt and ended up being sold to Potiphar, a high-ranking Egyptian, and worked his way up to head of the house. The Bible tells us that Potiphar could see the favor of God in Joseph in everything he did. Joseph found favor with Potiphar and became one of his most trusted servants.

Potiphar's wife tried to seduce Joseph. When he rejected her attempts, she falsely accused him of rape. Joseph, though innocent, was cast into prison.

While in jail, Joseph interpreted the dreams of two of his cellmates, which later proved to be true. One of his cellmates was released back into the free world and became the king of Egypt's cupbearer. Two years later, the king began having troubling dreams and the cupbearer (Joseph's former cellmate) remembered Joseph and his gift of dream interpretation. He told the king about him.

Joseph interpreted the king's dream, was released from prison, and he was made a ruler in Egypt (second only to the king).

A famine (part of Joseph's interpretation of the king's dream) happened a few years later, and Jacob (Joseph's father) sent ten of his sons to Egypt to find food. When the ten brothers got to Egypt, they bowed before Joseph, requesting food. They didn't even recognize him.

Joseph revealed who he was, then forgave his brothers and their dad. Then, all the brothers moved to Egypt to be with Joseph, who realized the dream had seemingly brought on his doom, yet proved that he would rule over his brothers.

When God gives you a dream, that doesn't necessarily mean it's going to happen right away. In 2009, I had a dream. At the time, it was the most vivid dream I'd ever had. In it, I was riding in the car with my cousin when suddenly, my wrist caught fire. I rubbed my wrist on my clothes to try to put it out, but then my whole body caught fire. I jumped out of the moving car and started running to the grass. I rolled around in the grass as the sun was setting and it started getting dark. When I tried to get up to head back to the car, I saw hundreds of mannequins wearing black t-shirts lying in the grass. All of the t-shirts had different words on them. But I was drawn toward three particular ones, which had the words:

> ✓ Business
> ✓ Ministry
> ✓ Writing

As I kneeled down to pick up one of the three mannequins, I woke up.

I felt like God was saying, "You don't have to choose. You can do all three." There were hundreds of mannequins. Those mannequins represented the different gifts God had given me. What I realized was that I would never have seen my potential had I not gone through the fire. That dream was in 2009, before I'd opened any store. Everyone tried to put me in a box by saying, "You're going to be a preacher." But there's no limit to what I can be with God and through God. Sometimes, people can't operate outside of the titles that others have put before them or that they have put upon themselves. I knew I'd much rather be relevant in the marketplace than the pulpit. I had the dream, but my life didn't reflect it at the time.

Because I didn't have anyone to speak to my entrepreneurship, I started straying away from it. I didn't come from a family of entrepreneurs in the technical sense. Though many of my family members hold the qualities of entrepreneurship, and many of them even started their own side businesses, they've never fully yielded to that call. Even though I'd had a business since the age of eight, by the time I got to high school, I tried to fit into the mold of society and the norm of my family.

Everyone tells you, "Go to school. Get a good job and follow your passion." But that just didn't feel right for me. I went through an identity crisis because, although I had been operating in my entrepreneurial gift from a young age, I still struggled to find what my "career" would be. Did I want to be an architect, a judge? Maybe I could study psychology. All of these thoughts stemmed from the pressure to pursue opening a business, which sounded great, but could only exist as a sort of side dish for my "career." There were too many people giving me well-intentioned advice. Their words were getting mixed up in my many thoughts. I needed some space to figure things out. The day after my high school graduation, I left Detroit. I moved to Texas.

> Changing location doesn't change who you are on the inside.

Many people didn't know this at the time, but I left

Detroit because I was battling depression. I thought leaving would set me free. But, soon after arriving to Texas, I realized I was still depressed. I was still confused. I still didn't know who I was. It took time, but I realized changing location doesn't change who you are on the inside. I had to deal with the internal battles. No matter where I was, nothing would change until I had a mindset shift.

ANOINTED WITH THE HOLY SPIRIT

In my second book, *Identity Crisis: The Final Verdict*, I talk about my battle with nine different identities and my overcoming them. I faced doubt, depression, low self-esteem, fear, anxiety, manipulation, lust, procrastination and anger.

The first year after leaving Detroit, while battling depression, I attended Wayland Baptist University to pursue a degree in business. That was a very tough time for me because I was still trying to find myself. Discovering who I was in a new place was difficult because everything was unfamiliar. I didn't have anything familiar to turn to for false comfort. In the scheme of things, it was life-changing, but I did not realize that at the time. I made it through my first year of college. But when I came home to Detroit for summer break, I had already decided that I didn't want to go back to Texas, deeming it depressing. But it wasn't Texas that was depressing. It was me. I was the cause, the culprit, of the depression.

> One of the greatest things to ever happen was leaving my comfort zone.

After three months of being back in Detroit, back in my familiar place, I still had a decision to make. With every fiber of my being, I was convinced that I would never go back to Texas. If I had to deal with constant battles, I'd at least want to deal with those things in my comfort zone. But even though everything in my body was telling me not to go back to Texas, there was a part inside, nagging me to go back to the Lone Star State. It was a feeling I couldn't shake.

Years later, as I reflect on this time, I realize the Holy Spirit was speaking to me. I was at a crossroads where I had to decide if I wanted to embrace it or reject it. To be honest, one of the greatest things to ever happen was leaving my comfort zone because it forced me to deal with myself. It forced me to view things differently and think differently. Though it was a painful process, it was necessary for what God called me to become.

The anointing isn't just some fancy way of being called into the limelight to shine before the world with great influence. It's about enduring hardships and struggles, and stripping yourself of your desires in order for God to fill you with His purposes and plans. Then, He can redeem you so that you can then turn and redeem those around you.

None of us like to endure bad times, and none of us want to go through challenges in life. But it's those challenges that make us stronger. It is in those challenges that we find our strength. It is in those challenges when we grab hold of our purpose. At the end of every tussle, we release the things we don't need and we grab hold of the things we do need to propel us forward – launching us into who God called us to be before the foundation of the earth.

CHAPTER SIX
PUSHED INTO PURPOSE

> For still the vision awaits its appointed time; it
> hastens to the end - it will not lie. If it seems slow,
> wait for it; it will surely come; it will not delay.
> —Habakkuk 2:3

I couldn't shake the feeling that I needed to go back to Texas. Three days before classes were beginning, I realized I had no choice but to surrender to the lead of the Holy Spirit. I'm often amazed with how God orchestrates our lives. Even when we don't understand the fullness of what He has planned for us, once we are obedient to His voice, He is able to do the unimaginable. And although I'd left Detroit the second time around with a fight, I'm glad I did leave. I look back now and I am truly grateful that I was obedient because God soon revealed to me exactly what He had in store for my life.

During my first year in Texas, I realized God had already started stripping me of religious routines. This is when I really began developing a relationship with Him. Three short months after returning to Texas, my faith was challenged like never before. It was during a time I believe was one of the most critical and pivoting points in my life.

It all began with the opening of my first kiosk in the mall. One day while casually walking around the mall, the vision hit me to open a Christian apparel store in the center of the building. I often hear how people talk about God speaking to them, and showing them what to do and how to do it. But I had never experienced a yearning so strong to do anything in my life. But, in this situation, I could literally see things exactly the way they needed to be done. I didn't have any money, but I went to the mall office to inquire about space.

> I heard the voice of God telling me, "If you invest your faith, I'll take care of the rest."

CAN'T SHAKE THE FEELING

Back in Detroit, a few years prior to this, I used to sell a few t-shirt designs out of the trunk of my mom's 1997 Nissan Maxima, thinking it was a cool way to share the gospel and to make a few extra bucks. But I'd put that on the back burner to go away to college. I remember going home from the mall that night and I just couldn't shake this feeling that I was supposed to be in that mall. I was supposed to open a store. I went over every excuse in my head as to why I couldn't do it. Yet, I still heard the voice of God telling me, "If you invest your faith, I'll take care of the rest."

With all of 38 cents in my bank account, I called my mom and asked her to ship me all the shirts I had left in her basement. I could hear my mom chuckling, but she did as I asked because she was long used to me and my witty, impulsive ideas. After rummaging through second hand stores and retail store dumpsters for clothing racks, I gathered my four dozen shirts and I approached the mall with my idea.

I went to the mall management office and walked in with full honesty and confidence. Wearing a black business suit and tie, I could feel their eyes upon me as soon as I entered the room. I wanted to catch their attention and ensure that they would take me seriously, especially because I was only nineteen years old. These were people in their 30s and 40s who had worked their way up the ladder. They sat quietly to listen to what I had to say, but little clues let me know they weren't happy to be there. One man kept looking at his watch. Another kept checking his cell phone. One woman sat completely still, except for one high-heeled foot that was tapping the floor rapidly.

I could feel beads of sweat on the back on my neck. On top of a less than enthusiastic audience, I also had to be transparent in the sense that I didn't have the finances. But I put my shoulders back and stood tall because I had full confidence in my ability to create a profit, should I be provided the right opportunity.

After pitching my idea, the leasing manager handed me an application and told me, "We're not supposed to do this, but there's something about you … " The woman stopped tapping her foot and stood up to shake my hand. The men nodded their heads and congratulated me on my presentation. Because of my preparation, public speaking skills and unwavering assurance, they were willing to give me a chance.

But they were also very curious to learn about my merchandising plans.

The general pitch to open a new store in a mall includes a prototype of what the store may look like. So, I put together a store in my aunt's living room and took pictures. I had to see it before I could sell it. I had to build the vision before I could see the vision come into fruition. I used these pictures and my t-shirts to present my idea to the mall staff.

I believe that the mall managers were able to look past my obvious lack of resources and take a chance on me. They were impressed with my presentation because of the favor of God, merged with my creativity and relentless faith.

I still remember the day the mall manager called me to tell me that my concept was approved by corporate. The way was clear to open my first store. I'll never forget the feeling of accomplishment that arose from that phone call, which was soon followed by nervousness and inadequacy. I was literally stepping into something much bigger than I had ever imagined.

Often when great things happen, we are met with two sets of feelings. I'm sure you've experienced excitement and accomplishment, as well as doubt and fear, almost in the same moment. However, never let fear rob you. Like the preacher Joyce Meyer always says in her sermons, "Sometimes you have to *do it afraid*." Just three short weeks after approaching the mall with my idea, I was able to gather $3,000 (which still wasn't enough in technical standards to open a fully operational business in a major shopping center). But with faith, I stretched it and made it work.

The original plan was for our 12x12 kiosk to be open for exclusively the holiday season, as it was the highest traffic point of the year. God saw beyond my initial two-month plan, though. While we opened in November of 2011, by February of 2012, I'd sold enough t-shirts to be able to move into a full in-line store, which was 10 times the size of my initial 144-square foot kiosk.

The name of the store in 2012 was *Religious Expressions*. Hindsight is of course always 20/20. It isn't out of line to note how *Religious Expressions* had manifested the business plan I'd once written in high school. It's almost like God had me script out the vision, without knowing I was willing it into existence. I now make the joke that had I known I was writing my business into being, I would have written higher sales numbers. Needless to say, I had experienced so much growth and favor that by 2013, I'd opened a second location in Amarillo, Texas.

> I didn't have to choose business over ministry, or ministry over business.

In every venture, there are learning curves. It seemed that I'd jumped too fast into the second location. The Lubbock store was somewhat carrying the store in Amarillo, which wasn't making enough money. I eventually closed the Amarillo store, and we moved into a bigger store in Lubbock. We ended up staying in Lubbock through 2014 and 2015.

GOD KNOWS MY PURPOSE

While business was good, I knew that *Religious Expressions* was more than just a business; it was my ministry. I could fill a whole book detailing the supernatural encounters we witnessed throughout the years. Rather than sales transactions, we saw people give their lives to Christ right in the store. We witnessed the prayer and encouragement in the testimonies of the tens of thousands that flowed in over the years, validating our sharing the gospel of Jesus Christ in the most untraditional of atmospheres. I truly believe that a major part of my purpose is to share the gospel of Jesus Christ in untraditional, uncommon places, in an untraditional way. My "pulpit" is definitely in the marketplace. I didn't have to choose business over ministry, or ministry over business, because God gave me the gifts and ability to do both. He has shown me over and over my true authority when I walk in the fullness of all He's gifted and called me to do.

Many times, I've wondered what in the world He had in store for me – like when our store flooded that first time because of a sewage line. I talk about the obstacles I faced in chapter one, and I am grateful for the success that came out of the chaos, even though it was tough to keep a positive attitude as I watched my business floating in a downward spiral. But, with God's help, we were finally able to reopen the store after a six-week repair closure, despite not having any insurance compensation.

Up through September, October and November of that year, business was slow and complicated. Yet, the grace of God led people to the store, seemingly out of nowhere. I was suddenly able to catch up on the store's bills after having been behind on three months of rent. I looked forward to moving to a prime location in the mall in the next month just before the holiday rush.

So, why did I have to experience that second flood just when things were getting good?

What I now know is that God allowed the flood, not to discourage me, but to show me that I was trying to build a house where He intended for me to only pitch a tent for a season. A lot of times, when things start to work out, we get comfortable. His Word says a good name is more desirable than riches. So, yes, I had to leave with a clean name. But God never intended for me to stay there permanently. He had something so much greater in store for me. God is all about stewardship. He couldn't let me walk away, owing money on the store. That wasn't going to bring glory to His name. But He allowed everything to be paid up, yet shut down, so He could move me to the next level - the next location - with a good name and no debt.

In December of 2015, I was forced to close down the store. I felt that closure in the pit of my stomach, but I knew there had to be a reason. I didn't want to sit and sulk, or listen to my thoughts that told me I had failed. I shooed away the

> Instead of letting myself sink into depression, I spent time seeking God's face.

voices that tried to tell me I couldn't run a business or that I should just go get a normal nine-to-five job, like everyone else I knew.

Instead of letting myself sink into depression, I spent January and February of 2016 seeking God's face. I had to find out what I should do next. I had to take time to be still and strategize. I didn't make announcements. I didn't make rash decisions. I simply sought after instructions from God before I decided to leap into where He was calling me to go next. I knew I had a purpose and that God would keep showing me my path. No one knew that I was taking a break. It was I who had to stop and ask God, "Where do I go from here?"

CHAPTER SEVEN
38 CENTS AND
A PLANTED SEED

> And when the LORD your God brings you into
> the land that he swore to your fathers, to
> Abraham, to Isaac, and to Jacob, to give you–
> with great and good cities that you did not
> build, and houses full of all good things that
> you did not fill, and cisterns that you did not
> dig, and vineyards and olive trees that you did
> not plant–and when you eat and are full.
> –Deuteronomy 6:10-11

While they didn't know it, there were many entrepreneurs in my family. Both sides of my family had entrepreneurs who had never fully walked the path. While they could hustle, their part-time hustles never evolved into full-time businesses. It should have been a legacy passed down to generation after generation. Instead, it was like a seared dream. I'm sure they dealt with everyday issues, like paying the bills, putting food on the table, and keeping that nine-to-five job. Then, there were even deeper issues, like the lack of startup money and maybe a lack of faith. I learned that whatever obstacles my parents or grandparents didn't defeat, I had to fight, whether they were of this physical world or from the spiritual realm.

In the Bible, we read of a young Hebrew boy named Moses. During the time of his birth, the king ordered that all baby boys born be killed. But Moses' mother put him in a basket in a river, and the king's daughter found him and raised him as her own.

PICKING UP THE MANTLE

Moses was a Hebrew boy, but he was raised as an Egyptian prince. While he'd been born a slave, he was raised as royalty. He grew into a man and set the children of Israel free. While he did not see The Promised Land, he was responsible for the freedom of tens of thousands. Although he knew he would not see the promised land, he'd already trained Joshua to pick up the mantle.

I truly believe that, though many in my family didn't walk in the fullness of faith to carry out the visions and dreams they had, they instilled in me what they had learned. Like

Moses to Joshua, they gave me a mantle to carry – allowing me to see new levels of greatness in business and ministry.

In Luke 21:1-4 (MSG), the Bible talks about how Jesus saw rich people dropping offerings in the collection plate. When he saw a poor widow put in two pennies, he said, "The plain truth is that this widow has given by far the largest offering today. All these others

> Once Moses moved in faith, he realized that everything he needed was already inside him to succeed.

made offerings that they'll never miss; she gave extravagantly what she couldn't afford—she gave her all!"

Ironically, we measure the greatest offerings or wealth by the largest quantity, not quality. If someone who makes $100,000 a year gives $1,000, it may seem large in the scope of things. However, if someone who makes $5,000 a year gives $500 in an offering, the person who gave the $500 is actually the person who has given more. It's important to give at the collection plate because, besides supporting our ability to go out into the marketplace, it also gives you a chance to offer your gratitude. But more important than just dropping money in the collection plate is offering your life to be used by God for His purposes and plans.

When God spoke to Moses at the burning bush, and God gave him an assignment, Moses didn't feel like he had what he needed. He didn't feel like he qualified. And yet, once he moved in faith, he realized that everything he needed was already inside him to succeed.

FAITHFUL ACTIVATION

The day I walked around the mall, and the Holy Spirit laid it on my heart to open my first store, I had 38 cents in my bank account. But after yielding to the call, and giving God my yes, I quickly realized that my faith was the activation for everything I needed to begin my journey. Just like Moses was not raised with or by his biological family, I, too, had to get away from my family. I didn't need to leave them in literal terms, but I had to get away from the traditional mindset.

I was born an entrepreneur, but raised with the state of mind to go to school and get a job. The fight inside of me didn't release until I stepped into the fullness of who I was born to be. I had to migrate to an unknown land. Just like the children of Israel and Moses wandered around the wilderness for 40 years, in an unknown land, when I moved to Texas, I felt like I was in a wilderness. I knew God told me to relocate, and He always gave me manna for the day. But it didn't make the daily discomfort any easier.

While Pharaoh and his men chased away the children of Israel, the Lord parted the Red Sea and allowed them to cross on dry land. But when Pharaoh and his army tried to cross that same dry land, the Lord allowed the water to consume them, preventing them from reaching the other side. If a slave escapes, but their master is chasing them, they're still a slave. They still have the mindset and mannerisms of a slave; they are still running. The journey the children of Israel took to the promised land was supposed to take 11 days. However,

> God did <u>not</u> tell us we aren't good enough to do more than live as a slave.

because of their mindset, they wandered, going in circles, in the wilderness, for 40 years. Essentially, it took one day to get the Hebrews out of Egypt, but 40 years to get Egypt out of the Hebrews. How many of us set out on a journey, but then we procrastinate and we allow our insecurities to stagnate our process to our own promised land?

BATTLING THE MINDSET

God did not tell us we aren't good enough to do more than live as a slave. We are taught early by well-intentioned parents, family members and teachers how to act, what to say, and how to live. It's important to learn the lessons of not touching a hot stove or running across a busy street. But many such lessons beyond that tend to strip us of who we really are.

Entrepreneurship, or stepping out in any area of obedience to God, has been much like that journey of the children of Israel. I still allowed my insecurities and my mindset to hold me back at times. While, just like the children of Israel, God has provided for me at every turn, I have still had doubts and bouts of stagnation at certain periods in my journey.

So, how do you change your mindset? How do you get past those doubts? By quieting your mind and listening to what God is telling you. Recognize when your thoughts are not beneficial and realize that they are just thoughts, not facts. Just because your brain tells you you're going to fail does not mean it's true.

My first day of business, I got dressed and ran to the store, knowing that I would sell a million t-shirts. Yet, on my very first day, after an eleven-hour shift, I didn't sell one thing. I remember saying, "God you told me to step out and do this!" The enemy immediately told me, "No one's gonna buy anything! You're stuck in a three-month lease and you owe the mall money."

So, fear set in.

I had to pull myself up and muster up enough courage to go back the next day and open my doors. My very first customer, John and Valentina Allen, came into the store all the way from New Mexico. Valentina wanted a medium t-shirt, but I didn't have a medium. They wanted to buy a copy of my first book, *Deliverance through Expression*. But when John pulled out his credit card, I didn't have a credit card processor. They left the store with nothing.

So, instead of making my first sale, I had to forfeit it because I didn't have what the customers needed. I was ill-prepared. Fortunately, they came back an hour later after going to the ATM to get cash. They bought four t-shirts, a tote bag and a book.

John asked, "Are you the owner of the store?"

"Yes, I am."

"Do you mind if we pray for you?"

When they prayed, they spoke to the spirit of fear and the spirit of inadequacy position, and told me that God was about to bless the store. They told me I would see the sudden increase.

> I walked in the overflow of God's promises.

On the third day, a group of high school students came into the store. They bought over $800 worth of product, running me out of stock. At the time, I didn't have much inventory. I'd only started the store with four dozen t-shirts. By that weekend, I had to order more stock and I had the money to do so. From that point on, I walked in the overflow of God's promises. But, just like the widow who gave two pennies in an offering, when I gave all I had, God honored my faith. It's not about giving all your money or earthly possessions; God is the creator of all things. It's about giving yourself fully to your purpose.

Just like Moses had to redeem the mantle of his own people, I felt like I had to redeem the mantle of entrepreneurship and wealth that was in my family all along. Although Moses didn't see the promised land, he'd deposited enough in Joshua for him to complete the assignment.

Many of my family members started several small businesses, yet never saw them come into full fruition and flourish. I believe one of the reasons was because they didn't have the validation, tenacity or drive to finish or create full blown businesses. It was difficult, likely because since they were chartering unknown territories, nobody knew how to speak into them and cultivate them. However, the seeds they sowed into me at an early age were enough for me to pick up the mantle and run with it—right into successful full-time entrepreneurship. I have never worked a corporate job. All I know is full-time entrepreneurship. Though this journey isn't always a breeze in the park, I know it's my calling and I will embrace it until I see nations changed.

CHAPTER EIGHT
A NEW LEVEL ...
A NEW NAME

> Behold, my covenant is with you, and you shall
> be the father of a multitude of nations. No
> longer shall your name be called Abram, [a] but
> your name shall be Abraham, [for I have made
> you the father of a multitude of nations. I will
> make you exceedingly fruitful, and I will make
> you into nations, and kings shall come from you.
> —Genesis 17:4-6 (ESV)

During my short sabbatical from business, after the second flood, I spent those few months truly seeking God for direction. I tried to understand exactly what He had in store for the next season of my life. Never negate the time spent in God's presence. What I've come to realize is that entrepreneurship is just as much spiritual as it is natural. It is God who gives wisdom, strategy and vision. So often, as entrepreneurs, our ambitions tend to overshadow seeking God for direction concerning our businesses.

After the year of hardship and struggle, mall management promised to finally move me back into a prime traffic area of the shopping center. They gave me three months of free rent, and even offered to help me market the store. So, imagine how I felt after finally catching up on rent and having some space to breathe again. Just when I thought things were going my way, I walked into the second flood. I won't pretend that I felt peace at first, and I won't pretend that I didn't use a few choice words with God. But I will say that after the tears dried, after the frustration faded, and after the noise ceased, I had to pray and be still.

I will never be one of those "Christians" who pretends that I don't have my moments where doubt and fear get the best of me. I won't pretend that I don't have those moments where I'm mad at God because things didn't pan out the way I expected them to. I won't even try to give you the illusion that I wasn't ready to give up in this moment. But once again, the resilience wouldn't let me fall.

> I like to think of the word *faith* as a verb because faith is action.

TRYING TO BE STILL

I don't know about you, but I hate being still. And I hate when folks try to get all deep in the middle of your situation and the only advice they have to give you is, "Be still." Being still goes against all my logic and personality. It goes against the entrepreneur in me that always has to be working and achieving and moving. But, in this situation, being still was the only thing I had left to do. I like to think of the word *faith* as a verb because faith is action. Anyone around me will tell you I live by the Scripture in James that tells us faith without works is dead. But what I realized during this particular defining moment in my life was that my true work was to be still and listen. It took an incredible amount of work for me to do that. I felt like I needed action because here I was, three days before the end of 2015, feeling like I was back at square one.

Oftentimes, in the quiet moments, God reveals what is next. As we are reflecting and shutting out everything around us, the answers will come. During this time of being still, I began reflecting back to 2013 when I visited Dallas, Texas and fell in love with the culture and business landscape. Maybe part of it was because I was born in Los Angeles, California and raised in Detroit, Michigan. Both are major cities and part of my genetic makeup was being a city boy.

Whatever the case, I felt such an urge to open a store in the Dallas-Fort Worth Metroplex. Doing so would give me access to the nearly seven million people that lived in the region, and would give me the opportunity to spread the gospel at large. When I went to survey the land, I felt exactly like Joshua and his spies. They surveyed the land God had promised them and reported back that they saw giants. Joshua sent his spies out to survey the promised land so they could prepare themselves to overtake it.

Essentially, I visited Dallas to appraise the land in 2013, but I felt unequipped and unworthy of being amidst all the greats. The malls were next level and the prices were quadruple. It was an entirely different world from the small towns with populations under 200,000 that I had operated all my other stores in. But the desire remained in my heart to one day see my business emerge in that territory.

It took nearly three years to finally see that unfold. But after enduring the flood and being still – for at least a little while – I was able to really figure out what was next. I spent a month of fasting, praying, seeking God and going through plans with the current mall management. Then, they estimated it would take another month or two to have my store open again and be ready for business. They upheld their promise to move me back into the prime area; however, the store that was promised to me had also been damaged by the storm, and would not be available right away.

Things seemed to be lining up properly but, during my prayer time, I felt the Holy Spirit shift things and release me from the old (everything I knew) and into the new. I felt such a pressing that now was the time God was releasing me to go to Dallas and embark upon a new journey.

For the past four years, all I'd known was *Religious Expressions*, and here God was calling me into something totally new and redefining. I remember going back and forth with God about my finances and, in that moment, I was reminded that I had more than *38 cents* – what I originally started with – so I had more than I needed. Here I was, at another moment of surrender. Only this time, things were extremely different. It was almost like the moment I surrendered, God not only opened doors, but He took them off the hinges. I knew without a shadow of a doubt that they were meant for me to walk through boldly and suddenly.

> We wait on God to give us clear signs of our next move when He is really waiting on us to take the next steps.

Oftentimes, we find ourselves waiting on God to give us clear signs of our next move when He is really waiting on us to take the next steps toward our desires. Once we do that, He can then activate the provision we need in order to go forth. The moment I made the decision that I was ready to release fear and charter new territory by planning the opening of a new store in Dallas was the moment that God released the provision for it to come forth.

It was my appointed time. God was ready to change my name and change my identity. He was ready to give me a greater assignment.

THE BIRTH OF 3:16

In the Bible, whenever we find that God changed someone's name, it was usually to establish a new identity. It was a prophetic decree of a shift in destiny. In the book of Genesis, we see God changed Abrams name to Abraham. Abram meant exalted father. Abraham meant father of many nations. During my waiting period, I remember the Holy Spirit whispering to me "Religious Expressions spoke to where you were, but 3:16 speaks to where you are going." *Global!*

> The brand failed to represent a genuine relationship with Jesus Christ.

Not only did the command come to change my name, but I also had to change the entire way I did business. For five plus years of business, I always brought and sold other people's t-shirt designs. I had made a few of my own designs, but I was never fully confident enough in my ability to create. *Religious Expressions* was a hodgepodge of t-shirts, gifts, Bibles, music and more. But, to be completely honest, I was never really happy selling that stuff because it spoke to religion, not faith. It failed to represent a genuine relationship with Jesus Christ.

It's easy to slap a Scripture on a shirt with a cheesy slogan and get a religious crowd to wear it. But I believe God gave me a vision and a mandate to create something that spoke to the lifestyle of a believer - something refreshing, but fashionable enough to spark a global movement in sharing the gospel of Jesus Christ. And so, *3:16 (3:16 Collection)* was born. It took overcoming fear, a lot of doubts and a lot of lies I told myself about what I couldn't do. I had to literally move past everything I had known about business. But the birth was amazing. Notice I didn't say *easy*. Spending time in God's presence came with refreshing strategies, innovation, and next level, game-changing ideas.

Never be afraid to change lanes. Don't become complacent with where you are at the expense of neglecting where God is calling you to be. New levels require releasing some things so that you can grasp hold of greater things. But, rest assured, God's plan is always bigger than anything we can imagine. Bigger than our fears, circumstances and resources, and He will always cause all things to work together for our good.

CHAPTER NINE
THE MARKETPLACE MANDATE

Imagine commerce bustling, doves flying around, smoked fish and leather-bound books. Envision sandal-beaten paths, the noise of haggling, shrewd negotiations and the exchange of goods and services. This is where Jesus was most often found during the time that He walked the earth.

> Jesus gave us a command to go out into the world and preach the gospel.

There is such a love that God has for the marketplace. Yet, when it comes to sharing the gospel, often we focus too much on the activities within the four walls of the church. We ignore the marketplace and the command that Jesus gave us to go out into the world and preach the gospel. The world, friends, definitely stems far beyond the reach of the physical church. The Bible calls Christians "the

Body of Christ." Essentially, we are the church and, like Jesus, our dominion, power and authority should freely flow wherever we go.

In the thirteenth chapter of Genesis, we encounter the patriarch, Abraham, his wife Sarah, and his nephew, Lot, leaving Egypt and going south. The Bible tells us that Abraham was extremely rich in livestock, silver and gold. His nephew Lot also had flocks and herds; he, too, was a wealthy man. Alongside one another, these men of great wealth traveled to Bethel. But the land couldn't contain them and support them because their possessions were too great. They had to spread out and go into different parts of the land.

The first time I read this passage, I got extremely excited because it gave me so much revelation about our existence on this earth as followers of Christ. A lot of times, we experience so much frustration in the church because we are all trying to dwell in the same place, not realizing that our "substances" together can't be contained in one environment of the church. We are afraid to leave the safety of the church and we have a natural fear of spreading out. But within the

> We hide behind our fear, not realizing the power or authority we have.

church, there is only so much space for us to coexist. The metaphorical "land" isn't enough to nourish or sustain our identities, talents and wealth.

Abraham, the father of Judeo-Christian faith, didn't have this fear. He was called a friend of God because of his faith. Like Jesus, Abraham lived and thrived in the marketplace. He had a trade, he negotiated land, he used wisdom to navigate challenging situations, and he was known as a man of substance.

Oftentimes, we hide behind our fear, not realizing the power or authority we have. Our authority as humans and believers is greater than we give ourselves and each other credit for. We can literally change the world. And that's not limited to singular parts of our lives. Our authority is so much greater when we exercise it in every realm.

GOD'S ENTREPRENEURS

Throughout the four gospels that chronicle the life of Jesus on earth, Jesus spent less time in the temple and the majority of His time in the marketplace. There, in the marketplace, He was often found sharing the gospel and performing signs, miracles and wonders. So, why do we as believers bind our ministries to just the body of Christ? It's as if our God-given gifts and talents only exist in private meetings of believers. Isn't the mandate to reach the world?

Have we considered the fact that most of Abraham's recorded life was not a "religious experience"? Abraham's authority on this planet came from "spreading his tent" and following God as the Lord led him to unknown places. Along the way, he grew in substance. Abraham was an entrepreneur, known by his contemporaries as a powerful man of valor.

> Entrepreneurship is an avenue in which we can, not only operate within the confines of our God-given gifts and talents.

I truly believe that entrepreneurship is a calling. I believe that entrepreneurship is an avenue in which we can, not only operate within the confines of our God-given gifts and talents — but it also brings us a freedom and access to resources that gives the kingdom of God a bigger reach on earth to see God's perfect will carried out.

In the book of Acts 18, Paul went out from the city of Athens and met a Jew named Aquila, and his wife Priscilla, who were tentmakers by trade. Paul was also a tentmaker. Through this marketplace encounter, he developed a working relationship with them.

We also read in the sixteenth chapter of Acts a story about a woman named Lydia, who was a dealer of cloth. What I love about the story of Lydia is that she hosted the apostle

Paul and the church at her home, and she was a big contributor (financially) to his ministry.

There are two significant things I want to point out. First of all, Paul, Priscilla, Aquila and Lydia were all entrepreneurs. When they operated in the vein of their gifts, it bought them a freedom to finance the agenda of heaven (sharing the gospel). The second significant thing echoes not only in the story of Paul, Priscilla and Aquila – but also in the story of Abram and Lot. Everywhere they went, the Bible deems us to know that they pitched tents.

WHY DO WE PITCH TENTS?

So, what is the significance of a tent? A tent is temporary provision. A lot of times, we are called to places on a temporary basis, but we try to build houses where God told us to pitch tents. The mandate from God was to preach the gospel across all four corners of the earth, which requires movement. But, too often, many of us become complacent and stand in our own way, not allowing God to move through us. The Latin word for tent literally means to stretch. It's not going to be comfortable to stretch. But every time we stretch, we make room for God to use us for His glory.

The anointing that God has placed on your life is too big to be confined to one space. The mandate is a global movement.

I often found myself analyzing why we have so many churches, but lack resources. Then I realized that we keep recycling the same dollar, expecting God to do a new thing, when He literally gave us the power to create wealth. Everyone wants to be a prophet, but they don't understand that prophets can't work without the profit. Our ministries are only as strong as the reach in our pockets. Don't get me wrong. It's never about the money; it's always about the mission. However, we are in the world and that's the currency and system of exchange. We have to operate in a way that we can comfortably grab hold of the resources we need in order to see God's will done on earth as it is in heaven.

MINISTRY AWAY FROM THE PODIUM

When God gave me the vision to open my store, I felt like He tricked me because, for so long, I ran from the ministry call on my life. I didn't want to stand in a pulpit. But God showed me that ministry doesn't just stem from a podium. As His vessels, we carry His glory inside of us. Wherever we are, we have a platform to share salvation.

I didn't realize how much ministry would go forth as far as opening my business in malls. Over the years, I've witnessed thousands of people giving their life to Christ inside of my stores. My employees and I have had the opportunity to pray and encourage tens of thousands of people, and the impact that these stores have had on the earth blows my mind. It warms my heart that God still moves, even in untraditional places.

There is a call for people like you and me to operate with our gifts and see others give their life to Christ in the marketplace. God is raising up people in every sector to walk in righteousness, extend our influence and reach the people in our various arenas of the world. Don't be boxed in. Don't neglect your passion because God can use the very thing you are passionate about to create a platform for your

> Go into the world and allow your passion to carry you to undiscovered territory.

ministry. I never thought in a million years that I could get paid to encourage people on a daily basis. I am able to bring hope and healing to people who desperately need it, but may never enter the local church.

I also create game-changing products in the midst of that. I get to live my passion daily. I get to witness the gospel, and I get to see people's lives transform right before my eyes. There is nothing more fulfilling than that.

What is the thing that you feel called to do, but neglect because you don't see how God can use it for His glory? Are you afraid to pitch your tent because you can't see a use for it in the church? If so, you are in the right mental state of mind. You simply need to go into the world and allow your passion to carry you to undiscovered territory. Along your journey in the marketplace, the place where you show the world your gifting, is where you will meet the people who you are supposed to influence. This is how we preach the gospel to all of the world.

WHERE DO YOU GO FROM HERE?

So, you may be wondering where to start. How do you begin to live a life that extends beyond modern day church life? First, find your passions and talents. Second, explore them and bring them to the world. Finally, everything we do should be done in excellence and for the glory of God.

Let's revisit our biblical friend Lydia. As we read of her legacy, we learn that she was a woman living in Thyatira. She is known as a "woman of purple." My dear reader, how do you become known by such a name? Lydia must have been passionate about the color purple! So much so that her passion caused her to become excellent in the production of the violet color spectrum. Lydia allowed her obsession with a color, like a painter with canvas, a baker with flour, or a beautician with tresses, to drive her to the marketplace.

Have you ever created something so good, that you had to share it with someone? Have you ever cooked a meal and found it so delectable that you were compelled to invite a friend over for dinner? In fact, you then tucked away your newfound recipe for future occasions. That is what it feels like to discover your passions and talents. It is the thing that's so good, you have to share it with someone else. I'd like you to consider that it is also the thing that is good enough to monetize for the spreading of the gospel.

Lydia was shrewd, driven by a desire to build wealth for herself and her family. Lydia was bold. She became a reputable business woman, whose life was canonized in the Bible for all of the world to learn from. Will you also consider with me that God held a special place of affection for Lydia's workmanship, bravery and marketplace know-how? When Paul encountered her, he did not meet a preacher, one who is well-versed in ancient Scriptures. Paul met an entrepreneur, perfectly positioned to be used by God in a way that would make her infamous.

Paul, the miracle worker and apostle, as well as the dejected and redeemed murderer, brought the power of the Word of God and his revelation. When Paul met Lydia in the marketplace, he exemplified such a grace and light that it compelled her to host Paul and the church. This shrewd business woman was capitalizing on an opportunity to encounter God. Lydia saw something so profound in Paul's life that it drove her to salvation. But, even more significant was that she didn't just convert and turn away. Her position as an entrepreneur, and the wealth she had amassed, gave her the unique ability to finance the ministry of Paul to give them a larger reach at spreading the gospel in her region.

So, take your passion, your business and your love for God beyond the church door and find your way to the marketplace. There are so many avenues to explore along your journey as you follow your passion and find more ways to share the gospel.

CHAPTER TEN
THY KINGDOM COME

The kingdom of God is in a season of sudden manifestation. More than ever, God is in search of those willing to walk boldly enough in their purpose to see His purpose fulfilled in the earth. For so long as a body of believers, we have missed the mark. We've gotten so tied up with religious rituals and routines at the expense of neglecting to operate in the fullness of God's plan for His children.

> "Thy kingdom come, thy will be done" are not just words we utter out of tradition.

"Thy kingdom come, thy will be done" are not just words we utter out of tradition. The meaning reflects the essence of our covenant with Jesus Christ. It's a mantra that brings life to not only God's perfect will – but it brings life to the roles we individually play within the confines of that assignment to the body of Christ.

I often question why God chose me to carry out such a great assignment. More often than I'd like to admit, I've asked God why He would give me such a large endeavor. But I realized it has nothing to do with my *ability*, but my *availability*. God only needs a willing vessel. Someone with a pure enough heart to choose His motives over their own – simply surrendered to Him.

Through the years, what I've realized is that God is very *intentional*. He uses every experience of our lives (good and bad) to mold us and shape us in a way that uniquely and perfectly qualifies us for the work that He has given to each of us.

> ## As each has received a gift, use it to serve one another, as good stewards of God's varied grace.
> –1 Peter 4:10

I love how this passage so eloquently commands us to serve one another with our gifts, all while abounding in God's grace. That same grace is responsible for making up for our failures, flaws and mistakes. Too often, we hold ourselves back from walking uprightly and boldly in our calling because we don't want to make others feel uncomfortable. But, in doing so, we hold thousands captive.

We should never minimize ourselves because it stops us from increasing God and bringing glory to Him through our gifts and abilities.

Don't get me wrong. It seems there can be a thin line between confidence and ego, but it's never about boasting in our abilities. It's about boasting of the God who gave us the gifts and abilities, and being confident enough to share those unapologetically with the world.

VISION

The Bible says in Proverbs 29:18, *Where there is no vision, the people perish.* My takeaway from this verse is different than many preachers who use this verse to promote their church vision agendas. But I truly believe the word "vision" in this passage refers to the revelation of God and who He is. Without the revelation of who God is, we lose sight of what He's charged us to do. When we lose sight of what He has called us to do, we perish (not physically, but spiritually).

Entrepreneurship is a calling, most often coupled with vision. Entrepreneurs have a certain way of seeing things beyond the surface, which many will deem innovation. But I like to think that alongside that innovation is also a strong dose of revelation. In Ecclesiastes 1:9, we read: *That which has been is what will be, that which is done is what will be done, and there is nothing new under the sun.*

The things we are discovering aren't necessarily new. But we are discovering new ways over old things, or rather unveiling purpose in things we may have looked at differently in the past. I believe God is raising up entrepreneurs to change the world through the marketplace. Even more, I believe that God is causing entrepreneurs to rise in various industries so that, ultimately, the gospel can be spread in every corner of the world.

MILLENNIALS ENJOY A PERSONAL RELATIONSHIP WITH JESUS

I often hear people discussing how millennials (a group I happen to be a part of) are falling away from church and God. The truth is we are not falling away from God or even church; we are just leaving religion and grasping the concept of a personal relationship with Jesus Christ. The face of church may be changing, and the method in which we reach people may be evolving. But, at the end of the day, the agenda is still the same – to share the message of faith, redemption and love with the world. We still share the story of how our Lord and Savior Jesus Christ died on the cross, was buried and resurrected on the third day to wash us clean of sin and give us an abundant life.

God's Word cannot return to Him void. So, any time God speaks, His words are obligated to perform. But, because He gives us free will, if we don't carry out the word, assignment or purpose God gave us, we will see someone else carry out the very thing God called us to do. It's never about us, but it is definitely up to us. I believe when we realize how many lives are tied to our obedience in fulfilling our purpose, we will feel the urgency to release fear and complacency and move forward in what God has called us to do.

When I finally got the release to shut down my stores in Lubbock and open my new business in Dallas, I experienced a level of fear I had never imagined. But the moment I released that apprehension, I was able to obtain the favor of God. There is something so magnificent about when that happens. The favor of God will cause things to align perfectly.

LEVELING UP MY FAITH

I remember when I approached one of the top malls in the Dallas region about opening a *3:16* store. I could never get a hold of anyone, so I told myself I wasn't worthy to be in that mall. It's astounding what kinds of negative thoughts go through our minds when things aren't going our way.

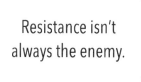

Resistance isn't always the enemy.

But then I received a call from that mall, letting me know that they had seen my store at another location. They were interested in my concept and wanted to bring it to their shopping center for a three-month trial during the holiday season of 2016. I had my meeting and my concept was approved. But weeks later, they rescinded my agreement due to a corporate merger that would be taking occupancy of the space I had signed an agreement for.

When I got that call, I blamed the devil. But I realized later that resistance isn't always the enemy. Sometimes it's God putting us under pressure to push us into the fullness of his plan. Essentially, I had settled for a small location in that mall that was definitely not up to par with what I knew I needed. I went along with it because I thought I could handle it in my own strength, when God was calling me to do something bigger than I was capable of by myself. I kept hearing the Holy Spirit say, "Put Jesus at the center of the mall," but I ignored the voice because I felt that was well out of my league. It was this resistance that left me with two options - give up or level up.

Eventually, I leveled up my faith, and the mall offered me a prime location that was greater than anything I could have ever imagined. My new store *3:16* was going to be placed in the center of one of the busiest malls in the Dallas Metroplex. Everyone would witness the favor of God on my business. But, more importantly, it would give us the opportunity to literally reach millions.

3:16 REPRESENTS JESUS

I remember the day the sign company came to install my signage at the new store. As they were lifting up the *3:16* logo over the storefront, I heard the Holy Spirit ask me, "What does *3:16* represent?" And I answered, "Jesus." I was drawn to the verse in the Bible where Jesus said, "If I be lifted from the earth, I will draw all men unto me." At that moment, things came full circle for me. As I was lifting, Jesus was drawing. He was drawing opportunities for me to share the gospel in a bold new way.

I'm not going to lie; I opened this store with my last $10,000. The mall manager didn't know that, or I'm pretty sure I wouldn't have even been given this opportunity because my rent was nearly that amount. However, God had a plan and He allowed favor to precede me. Everything I needed to open this store began to come together.

Needless to say, not only did I have my first ever six-figure sales month, but I saw hundreds of people give their life to Christ and thousands of people rededicate their life to Jesus Christ. Imagine if I had been disobedient and not answered the assignment with my, "Yes!" It would have not only affected me, but it would have impacted thousands of others. And in the process of doing the work of the Lord, He gave me a two-part reward. It catapulted my business to a new level and it also solidified my purpose, while leveling up my faith. The vision will always come with provision.

Another thing that took place was God showed me my worth. The store was now 100% my original designs, and it reminded me that God gave me a creative anointing. Though I doubted that people would like my original designs, not only did they like them – but many testified that it was like nothing they had ever seen. The support was tremendous.

> Stop comparing
> yourself to others
> and be authentic
> in what God
> gave you.

BE AUTHENTIC

I think we don't give ourselves enough credit when it comes to being innovative and having confidence in the ideas God gives us. We are always looking for a template or something to compare ourselves to. But the thing about vision is that, more often than not, you're a trailblazer — the first in your field to do something. Stop comparing yourself to others and be authentic in what God gave you.

When Moses built the ark, do you think he was looking around to see the other arks? No! They didn't exist; he was the first to do it. People thought he was crazy, but he walked in faith and confidence and did something amazing for his time. We can even bring this example more current and relevant to today. When Steve Jobs created Apple, he was blazing a territory that had never been chartered. But, in doing so, he changed the world. And you can and will change the world, too.

> Thy kingdom come, thy will be done,
> on earth as it is in heaven.

Remember your covenant with Jesus. Don't forsake the idea God has given you. It's bigger than you can imagine and you will miss out on something incredible if you ignore His support. Trust me - you are going to change the world.

CHAPTER ELEVEN
ESTABLISHING A KINGDOM BUSINESS

So, as entrepreneurs, how can we use our influence to affect and infect the world with change? How can we exercise dominion and use our businesses to the glory of God? For an aspiring entrepreneur, you may be asking how to even start a business. Let's take a look at the steps.

IDENTIFY YOUR GIFT

I believe the first step in establishing a kingdom business is to identify your gift. What is it that you are called to do? What is it that God gifted you with that you've always held a special passion for? For me, I always felt that encouraging people was what made me the most fulfilled and satisfied. I never believed that God could use that for His glory outside of the realm of preaching in a pulpit. But boy was I wrong. God has shown me that I can do both and, more often than not, they interconnect. I can run a successful business and still encourage people and share the gospel. So can you.

DEVELOP YOUR WHY

After identifying your gift, one of the most important steps is developing your why. Ask yourself why you are doing this. Starting a business is all about being the solution to someone's problem. This can be looked at in both a

> Starting a business is all about being the solution to someone's problem.

natural and a spiritual way. In the natural realm, your business can literally solve someone's problem. It can be as simple as a cleaning service that solves the problem of a busy family dealing with a dirty house.

But, in the spiritual realm, you may be the only encounter of Christ someone may ever have. Some people have never stepped foot into a church. Others have visited a church, only to walk away after a distasteful experience. Many will encounter you in your everyday business, which could lead to important conversations. Talking to you may inspire them to rekindle their relationship with God or develop one that they may have never had. Your why should never be because you want to make money. That's a natural part of business. Your why should always extend deeper than that.

SPEND TIME WITH HIM

The next important aspect is to spend time in God's presence. This is where we find instruction and confirmation. Too often we go to God in prayer to talk and list out all of our wants and needs, but rarely do we listen. Prayer is not always a petition. True prayer is a conversation. God wants to have a relationship with us, and

> God has not given us a spirit of fear, but of love, power and a sound mind.

relationships are mutually beneficial. But, as in life, the key to a successful relationship is communication. Sometimes the best prayers are just sitting in meditation, allowing God to speak to our hearts. For me, the best ideas I received have been during my times of worship and consecration.

SHAKE OFF THE FEAR

After you have identified your gift and calling, developed your why, and spent time in God's presence for instruction, the next step is the most critical. It's where most people fall away. Shaking off the fear! The Bible tells us in 2 Timothy 1:7 that God has not given us a spirit of fear, but of love, power and a sound mind. Fear is a natural reaction to things that are outside of our comfort zone and many times, outside of our control. But it's so important to avoid those kinds of pitfalls. You see, on the other side of our fears is destiny. So, shaking off fear is probably the most important part of the process in establishing a kingdom business.

BE AUTHENTIC

I talked about this step in the previous chapter, but it's so important to be you. Be true to who you are. Don't duplicate what others are doing. Trust what God has given you and always remain true to your vision. No matter how difficult it may seem, keep pushing, no matter what. Don't allow the world to cloud your vision, and don't let your lack of resources stop you. You may have to remind yourself many times, but be clear about what it is you want to do and be authentic.

HAVE RELENTLESS FAITH

> Prayer is the key, but *faith* is what unlocks the door.

For me, the next step came the easiest. But it may not be the same for you. You must have a relentless faith, no matter what. Whatever obstacles come your way during your business journey, always remain unwavering because faith will literally be the difference between failing and succeeding. In my business, I've faced things that would have caused the average person to give up. But my faith was always the push that kept me going. Prayer is the key, but *faith* is what unlocks the door.

ELEVATE OTHERS

Lastly, in the kingdom, it's all about elevation. Too many of us are scared to delegate and elevate others. But as you lift other people up, God elevates you. I don't know if it's a natural fear of others getting ahead of us, or lack of confidence that our businesses will never be good enough to require a team. But if you can achieve your vision alone, it's not big enough. True leadership is executed when those who follow are able to walk in a double portion of your wisdom. I've always enjoyed seeing others thrive off of my instruction and mentorship because it is how God intended leaders to live. And it is truly reminiscent of my apostolic mandate to raise up other leaders and entrepreneurs. Never be afraid of someone getting ahead of you. What God has for you is for you, and there is always room at the table for us all to eat.

USE YOUR INFLUENCE TO GLORIFY GOD

Once you are thriving in your business, you can be a source of influence to others out there. You don't have to preach to them or try to force people to listen to your message. It will come naturally as you do business with what you have to share with the world, how you conduct yourself and in conversations.

Of course my business is a little more obvious and directly related to His Word. But when you are helping others, your message will come through. And remember, we're in this to help. The way you respect people and treat your employees will also reflect your love for God. And again, lifting others up by offering mentorship or simple kindness will return rewards to you double fold. Even if you are not quoting Scriptures to someone, your actions will speak for the type of man or woman you are and will show what, and who, you believe in.

Throughout the day, you'll have conversations that may lead you to speak about your faith. That's when you'll share your message directly. People will see your success and want to know how you got to that point. That's an excellent time to reveal that your faith in God kept you going, in spite of the obstacles.

Sharing your gifts as an entrepreneur is a wonderful way to spread the Word of God in the marketplace. Once you know what you want to do and why, spend time in His presence and He will carry you through the difficult times. Always lift others up and never, ever doubt His love.

CHAPTER TWELVE
RUNNING WITH REVELATION

> Then he said to his disciples, "The harvest is plentiful, but the laborers are few; therefore pray earnestly to the Lord of the harvest to send out laborers into his harvest."
> —Matthew 9:35-38

The gospel according to Matthew as described in Matthew 9:35-38 paints a picture of Jesus traveling through the cities and villages, teaching, healing and sharing his wisdom with the community. Matthew records this passage, saying that Jesus had compassion for the crowds because they were helpless and ungoverned. He compares them to sheep without a shepherd. As Jesus travels and encounters these people, He makes a profound statement to the disciples: "The harvest is plentiful, but the laborers are few." Then he goes on to say, "Pray earnestly to the Lord of the harvest to send out laborers into his harvest." This is one of the most revelatory passages I've ever read, especially as someone who feels a strong calling to evangelism in the marketplace.

If we look at our landscape as people in the world, we have so many churches, so many missionaries, and so many people who feel called to preach. Yet, too often, we don't see the amount of churches correlating equally to the amount of people giving their lives for Christ and walking earnestly in love as He instructed the believers and citizens of His kingdom. I believe that if Jesus was to walk the earth today, it would be a mirror image of this passage in Matthew.

PRAY TO BRING LABORERS TO THE HARVEST

Jesus would probably tell us the same thing. But what exactly did Jesus mean by the harvest and the laborers back then, and how exactly can we apply that same scenario to modern-day culture? Today, the harvest represents the tools we have to minister with. If He came down to earth, Jesus would say that we have many beautiful buildings from which to worship, and numerous leaders within the churches, but not enough people taking that message out into the world. Then, He would instruct us to pray sincerely and thoughtfully for the guidance of His followers to step out of the churches.

I believe we have limited "ministry" to preachers, bishops and apostles — not realizing that every believer's duty is to share the gospel of Jesus Christ. Not just through our words, but through our talents, gifts and, ultimately, our lives. So many people have felt judged and abandoned.

> Reaching people is more effective when you reach them on their level, in their language, and in their culture.

They've experienced so much disdain within the "church" that we have lost our effectiveness in winning souls and sharing the gift of salvation with those around us. The message of the cross remains the same, but we've gotten narrow-minded when it comes to how we are supposed to truly reach others.

The harvest is huge. There are a lot of people to reach, yet the laborers are few because ministry has been reduced to those with titles and to specific atmospheres. But God is calling His generals to the marketplace. He's calling everyday people, like you and me, to walk in power and exercise our authority in the arenas in which we already have influence. To you, it may be a hair salon, a grocery store or on your job as a teacher. To someone else, it could be in a doctor's office, a laundromat or working as a mail clerk.

For me, it's been in the malls, in shopping centers and in boardrooms across the globe. Reaching people is more effective when you reach them on their level, in their language, and in their culture, versus trying to beat people over the head with terms they won't understand or inviting them to places they may never attend until they receive understanding and revelation on them. Because of your specific set of experiences in life, you are called to reach people I may not be effective at reaching, and vice versa.

YOU ARE A REFLECTION OF CHRIST

The ultimate reflection of our faith is not in our ability to recite Scriptures. It resides in our being and existence. St. Francis said, "We must preach the gospel at all times and, if necessary, use words." That literally means people should be able to look at you and see you're a reflection of Christ. What better way for your light to shine than to simply be in the places you are every day? Faith is not this complex idea we debate; it's a lifestyle. Faith should be shown in our everyday works.

This has been the most endearing revelation I've come to terms with in my life. God wants to use me where I am, as I am, with what I have. And the same goes for you. God wants to use you where you are, as you are, with what you have.

> God gave me relentless faith, courage and boldness to reach every goal and conquer every dream He has given me.

Wherever we go, we should carry with us authority and ability — authority to change lives, and ability to share God's love with everyone we encounter.

The past couple of years, I have not only been blessed to build an amazing store, but I've been fortunate enough to build a powerhouse brand, a movement and an avenue for believers and non-believers alike to gather and be inspired by the love that the gospel of Jesus Christ brings. I couldn't be more humbled with the results. And to think, this is only the beginning.

I remember selling t-shirts out of the trunk of my mom's car. I was just a 17-year-old boy with a heart to love people and inspire people, and share my experiences of how a radical God gave me relentless faith, courage and boldness to reach every goal and conquer every dream He has given me. I never got caught up on the destination. I just stayed the course and enjoyed the journey (and I am still enjoying the journey).

I obeyed the call to open that store with just 38 cents several years ago. Now, not only have I been afforded opportunities to send products across nations, but doors have opened for me that I never thought possible.

Earlier in the year of writing this book (January 1, 2018, to be exact), I was sitting in prayer and reflecting on the previous year, writing my goals and vision for the New Year. The first thing I wrote on my list was to travel to two countries. I then declared that 2018 would be the year of elevation and sudden manifestation for me.

Two weeks later, I received a call that changed my life. A man from South Africa had visited one of my stores in Texas while he was on a business trip to the United States and fell in love with my concept. More importantly, he was moved by my story. He reached out to me and invited me to travel to South Africa, all expenses paid, to share my story with a group of entrepreneurs. He also wanted to talk about expanding my brand to other countries.

Since 2013, I had been speaking the word *global*, not knowing exactly what that entailed. But that one word became my daily confession and sort of a prayer. The Bible talks about how God has given us the power to create with our mouths. I always tell people to be careful what you speak because it can be the thing that blesses you or curses you. I realized that trials would come and I would face tough times. But, even in those moments, I had to speak what I wanted, not what I felt. That is the power of faith.

Needless to say, I got to travel to South Africa and Dubai to share my story, and I am now in the process of expanding the 3:16 brand globally. I've received calls from Australia, Europe, Germany and many other countries ready to partner and take the marketplace by storm. I say all this not to brag and boast, but to show you that the dream inside of you is bigger than you can even imagine. All it takes is one step of faith, one moment of boldness, and some sacrifice. More importantly, authentically follow your heart and allow God to meet you, right where you are, with what you have.

THIS IS ONLY THE BEGINNING FOR YOU

Thank you for taking the time to read my story. I hope it has been inspiring for you and I've enjoyed sharing it. I'm a prime example of someone who takes their passion out into the marketplace and uses that avenue to share the Word of God. It's your turn to take your aspirations and turn them into something you can share — something that brings you joy and lets you help others.

So, it's time. Stop doubting yourself. Stop stressing over what you don't have. Don't argue for your limitations. I'm a living testament that whatever you don't have, you don't need. God has already given you everything necessary to achieve the dream deep down inside of you and see His purpose for you manifested.

If you have more than 38 cents, you have exactly what you need. All you have to do is watch how God will take that seed and spring forth a harvest beyond anything you could ever ask for, think of, or imagine. It's time for you to change the world. Are you ready to be sent out into the harvest?

The same God who took my 38 cents, and turned it into a multi-million dollar brand, is the same God who is ready and willing to do the same for you. Will it be easy? Nope! Will there be times you want to give up? Absolutely! But I promise if you stay the course, not only will your life change, but lives of those around you will be touched and changed. There is someone out there depending on your, "Yes!" in this moment to save their life.

What are you waiting for?

Store in Aunties Living Room

First Lease, First Day, First Store

Interior of
Religious Expressions

and

Worship Night

3 Months After Opening Religious Expressions

First 3:16 Store

3:16 Store–Center of Busiest Dallas Mall

Future 3:16 Conference Room

ABOUT JAYLEN

While many boys played with model cars, trucks and trains—he was working toward building an empire. From humble beginnings of selling items in his mother's basement and from the trunk of his car—to his undeniable success as a full-time faithpreneur, author and speaker, it's crystal clear that faith isn't just a principle to Jaylen LaGrande. It's a lifestyle. As the Chief Steward and Visionary of *3:16* (formerly *Religious Expressions*), he's committed himself to not just excellence in the marketplace and business—but marketplace ministry. Whether you catch him at a book signing, traveling the world to speak, or behind the counter at one of his locations for *3:16*, a Christian retail store, his message, his mantra and his mission remain the same—faith, hope and empowerment.

At the young age of 8, his passion for purpose fulfillment and business shined as bright as a 1,000-watt light bulb. After hanging flashlights from the ceiling to create spotlights, and building a small stage, he successfully sold tickets to his version of the North American International Auto Show, where he showcased his model car collection. Admission was only a quarter. By the age of 11, he was well on his way to becoming a successful entrepreneur through graphic design and his greeting card company. By November of 2010, Jaylen published a magazine that gained phenomenal success—so much so that it drew the attention of a buyer before the second edition and Jaylen sold all rights to the publication. But his love for design and writing was not lost in the sale—it was simply refocused.

In 2009, Jaylen published his first book, *Deliverance through Expression*, a short story with a collection of poetic prose. By the summer of 2012, his sophomore book project, *Identity Crisis: The Final Verdict* hit the shelves, and he couldn't keep copies on the shelves fast enough. His third project, 38 Cents, was released in the Fall of 2018. Featured on Fox News and other media outlets for his significant success at such a young age, Jaylen is adamant about customers walking away with more than just a great product. They walk away with empowerment. They walk away inspired. They walk away with a measure of undeniable faith to believe that if God did it for him, He can do it for them, too.

Jaylen studied business at Wayland Baptist University, and continues to grow his reach and ministry through 3:16—showcasing to others that when you truly believe, all things are possible!

For more information or for interviews, please visit www.jaylenlagrande.com, email info@jaylenlagrande.com or search *Jaylen LaGrande* on all social media outlets.

OTHER BOOKS
BY JAYLEN

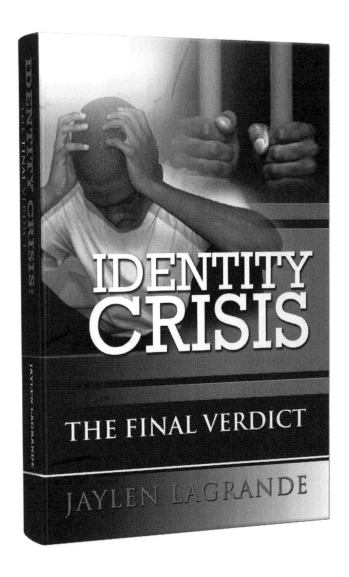

BOOKS BY JAYLEN CAN BE PURCHASED AT:

www.JaylenLaGrande.com